# GRAVITAS

*Volume 18 Issue 1*

Editor-in-Chief
## Andrew Lafleche

Andrew Lafleche, Editor-in-Chief
www.AJLafleche.com

Printed in the United States of America

First Printing: December 2018
Pub House Books
www.PubHouseBooks.com

ISBN-13 978-1-989266-08-3

# CONTENTS

Editorial Notes................................................................................................1

Part One ..........................................................................................................3

    Time Will Come.........................................................................................4

    Hunt Me Down ..........................................................................................5

    My Mother's Hands...................................................................................6

    Catch and Release .....................................................................................8

    Ascetic........................................................................................................9

    Last Summer............................................................................................10

    Within .......................................................................................................11

    Huxley's Daughter .................................................................................12

    Goodnight.................................................................................................13

    Idling ........................................................................................................15

    Fire............................................................................................................16

    Words Like Rain......................................................................................17

    Porcelain Truth .......................................................................................19

    Nothing.....................................................................................................20

    Between Haircuts ....................................................................................21

    My Name is Not Gregor.........................................................................22

    Walkthrough Inspection........................................................................23

Part Two .........................................................................................................25

    Los Arcos .................................................................................................26

    Fountain of Renouncement ...................................................................28

    Among the Core-fired Ashes of Faith ..................................................29

    Los Templarios ........................................................................................31

    The Weave of Heaven .............................................................................33

    My Movie of Prokofiev ...........................................................................35

    Jiving with The Wind..............................................................................37

    A Capitol March.......................................................................................38

    Bitter.........................................................................................................40

    The Waiting Room ..................................................................................41

    Mile Marker 154, Kingman Arizona......................................................42

    Frank.........................................................................................................43

    Love, Like a Skull....................................................................................44

    78th Avenue & Woodhaven Boulevard, Queens.................................46

    Skeleton ...................................................................................................47

    Atmospheric Depressions .....................................................................49

Part Three ............................................................................................51

    As We Go ........................................................................................52

    I Rode a Tortoise ..........................................................................53

    Delta Journal ................................................................................54

    Aylan Kurdi ..................................................................................55

    Abandoned ....................................................................................56

    Ingesting Eclipses ........................................................................57

    Was ................................................................................................58

    All That Summer ..........................................................................59

    The Catholic in Istanbul .............................................................60

    Downtime ......................................................................................62

    I Want to Ask My Mother ...........................................................63

    Little Girls and Alligators ..........................................................65

    To the Tarot Card Reader at the Kit Kat Club .........................68

    Vagabond Soul ..............................................................................69

    Shards ............................................................................................70

    Maybe It's Just Me .......................................................................71

Part Four ..............................................................................................73

    Hindsight .......................................................................................74

    Fajardo ..........................................................................................75

    Prostitute: San Francisco ............................................................76

    Metamorphosis .............................................................................78

    If We Could Only Slow It Down .................................................79

    Wounds ..........................................................................................80

    Beauty ............................................................................................81

    The Edge ........................................................................................82

    Moments and Mundane ...............................................................83

    Wild Air .........................................................................................84

    Destruction as the Cause of Coming into Being ......................85

    The Day Before We Left You ......................................................87

    When the Bank Says My Account Was Drained .......................88

    I Survived #METOO .....................................................................89

    And After the Accident ................................................................92

    The Cousins ...................................................................................93

Contributors ........................................................................................99

# EDITORIAL NOTES

THIS WILL BE BRIEF. I am not one for long editorial notes or editorial notes at all for that matter, alas, it appears I must write something. Here it goes:

I am fortunate to work with poets and writers from all walks of life, all over the world, individually, and as a collective. One of the common-most concerns I hear from aspiring writer's is, why would they submit their poetry to an anthology or magazine if they're not going to be paid for it? Although I don't share the same sentiments, I will address it by way of quoting Orson Scott Card. "Our objective as storytellers and writers isn't to make money – there are faster and easier ways of doing that. Our objective is to change people by putting our stories in their memory; to make the world better by bringing other people face-to-face with reality, or giving them a vision of hope, or whatever other form our truth telling might take."

This being said, I sincerely wish to thank each of the contributors whose work appears in this issue, and the hundreds of others who took the time and consideration to submit to this printing. Without each of your efforts, Gravitas would not be possible. Thank you.

Yours,
Andrew Lafleche
Editor-in-Chief

# PART ONE

*"quiver in the following breeze."*

## Time Will Come

When we won't be able to call
A fig tree a *fig tree*
A lemon tree a *lemon tree*

Or an orange tree an *orange tree*
Because a *willow tree* will
Take an offense

Cry discrimination
And demand
We call everyone a *tree*.

~Javed Latoo

## Hunt Me Down

If you want me now,
you better hunt me down.
I'm tired of chasing—
Kids, jobs, dogs with socks,
dreams.
Feel free to Three's Company me
and come knock on my door,
or do a Blondie and call me.
I'm not despondent,
I just need a rest.

I've chased all my life:
Boys, ice cream trucks,
the moon.
I will no longer run.
Not my knees, nor my heart
can handle the motion,
or the emotion of it.
I'll be lounging beneath
a Jacaranda tree,
seeing what comes for me.

~Lisa Poff

# My Mother's Hands

Sun spots, veins and bones,
all the fat of youth gone.
"My hands are never
gonna look like that,"
I thought to myself,
some twenty years ago,
when I took pride in
the fact that my bitten
nails had grown.

I kept them painted
every shade of red,
from tomato to ruby and blood,
with fancy names like
"Big Apple Red-headed Stepchild."

Sign me up for the degree needed
to name lipstick and polish.
I imagine them sitting around
some conference room table
laughing and drinking Starbucks.

I used to slather my hands in Vaseline,
and wear white cotton gloves to bed
like any good Southern woman.
My skin was soft as Snow
White and laced with crimson.

After years, dish soap, kids, sun,
and such lack of time
to even put on lotion,
I glance down upon
them and remember,
"My hands are never
gonna look like that."

I had been so sure.
But now I see....
They've become hers.

~Lisa Poff

## Catch and Release

Imprisoned, back of the mind they burn
truth seared memories clamor for release, but

my children;
too young to carry heavy burdens

my grandmother's bones;
too brittle for the weight of these transgressions

the sins of the father;
would break my father

so I leash the tongue, but
in my darkest hour, slip loose

lean down as the children sleep
brush wispy hairs from baby brows

kiss their soft cheeks and tell them
it's not the strangers they should fear

~Alia Wall

## Ascetic

all pageantry recoiled, the ballroom shrunk away
the celebration got smaller and smaller
streamers trailing confetti like exhaust
leaving you in a deep wood
with the far-off sound
of water
you remember then, suddenly
as lightning—
the scar on your hand cut through
the lines of your palm
and you took off, bounding
the earth rising
the wind pushing you along
in its wing
you made your way into the desert
burning
between you and your love.

~Jim Trainer

## Last Summer

"Yeah well
that was last summer,"
she sassed
and
goddamnit
she was right.
I watched her try on
a pair of pumps then
grind out a Lucky
and start a bath
we are moving forward now
me&her
I never thought I could
love somebody
someone
so much
and trolley cars
bang down Fillmore
as I lather up
look in the mirror
and watch her pull her stockings on
like victory.

~Jim Trainer

## Within

there is no moral or idea
no issue or umbrage
no campaign or crusade
that can make somebody disappear
the way that Black Ops in a country
at the edge of Western hegemony can

there is no politic, no Bible
no high flying flag
out on the street where I can see your eyes
in this hemisphere, the war is psychic
we wear each other down, castigate and
dehumanize in a "soap that never ends"
while over there the spit's turning
hunger mixes with ideology and plans
the next tragedy
they keep hitting closer to home
while we make a Budweiser commercial about it
keep our heads down, assume it's them, they're
the enemy

I am not innocent, you are not innocent
no one is innocent
and I'm weary
I spend as much energy avoiding you in the street
as it would take for me to help you
the world is getting smaller but you're
walking too close to me, buddy

back off.

~Jim Trainer

## Huxley's Daughter

this morning I want you palpably,
it runs from my gut followed by a rush of blood
I open the front door and a strong spring wind
has cleared the path of palms wrecked
in the rain that fell hot and fast this morning
I woke with the storm, in the lee hours
and felt the curve of you, deep in the crease
of my hips and deeper, that's what this ease
of connection is, like a magic you're here
a quick conjuring, I remember our every
conversation had with the whole body, the
intellectual sensuality, our whole heart in our palms
locked like two faces, over the
cool oasis of linen between us on
hot windy mornings like this one, that woke me
...and restarted this, fevering
there are paths that cut steeply and give rise
on Wheeling where we kissed and brushed red
dirt under giant Sequoias sighing, you
can see the Golden Gate like you're looking
at the end of the civilized world, the ocean
drops off into the wild, an expanse of self
I'd never felt before, and is stuck in where
my rib used to be, this sliver of you
gone but not gone, a hard laugh that softens
tears that widen and soak wet the corners
you're in the ether, Gemini, quick Mercury, the
vitreous of me, never touching down
a vapor a visage, you passed through but left
fine residue, the soft tissue of me tinged with you
my borders open the stretches of me wildly
overgrown and thriving in bloom

~Jim Trainer

## Goodnight

when I started out
they'd just taken our media away
and for that offense we
came together
and rousted the bastards out
we saw healthcare pass
same sex marriage
and medical marijuana
and when they took 'em down in Tripoli
and our media was back in our hands
there was a sense that the dark turns
the new century had taken
could be rolled back, we might win
we could live in a world without war and
undefined by race or sex—at least that's
what me&the liberals thought
maybe the terribly oppressed have
always known better
because
the ax has been swung back

we're living in a slow-motion sunset now
and the light's getting pale and thin
there's snow on the ground but it's
windy and warm
there are cities in the once greatest
country in the world
without electricity or drinking water
and countries
being bombed
to rubble

I'm glad of the Dalai Lama and
glad for these kids up there
making a change
but I can't rally, I can't hope

I can't find a plumb line through the madness
or see anything beyond this slow-motion sunset

I live out my days
in the grips of a roaring anxiety
I feel this last swing out acutely
we're moving toward catastrophe
and War and the panicked chicken
citizens
have spotted blood

this is the end of my intermittent valiance
what I've struggled against for the entire
of my adult life
has been lost, I'm going dark
for the last time
I'm going dark
goodnight

~Jim Trainer

## Idling

The place smelled of fire
and water.
Jimmy and I
were hired to rip the wall
boards
and floors
from their places and
discard them.

We loaded the truck
all morning,
took on the smell
of wet, burnt wood. Jimmy

stopped the truck at a red light,
and ran to a place
to buy beer for himself. I sat
at the light and ignored the honks
other drivers thought would move
the idling truck
forward.

They didn't know
who they were dealing with. A man
with a desperate
need
trumps

the sounds the world makes.

~Gary McCarty

## Fire

How can one write
about the dead, those
who sat beside you,
told stories, held your hand?

You remember their chilled skin,
their hands moving excitedly
as they looked at you and told their tales, sipped
their tea and laughed.

These moments leave
as the last log in the fire burns down
to red embers.

Memories
of the once living
are untrustworthy, filled
with lost hopes
as we stoke the fire,

dreaming.

~Gary McCarty

## Words Like Rain

Dripping clear
off the awning of a sidewalk cafe,
the rain
puddles alongside the table
where we sit talking,
sipping hot coffee.

You say the day
has been hard and
this conversation also hard, you
want to leave, my words of explanation,
words for the moment, you say,
not real,
like the cold rain
is real,
not visible,
like the smoke spiraling up
from your cigarette
is visible, or your breath, or

your fear.

You want to go home,
alone,
settle in the tub,
bathe,
and shave your legs,
rub them with cream,
lie on the couch and read,
talk to no one,
because you have no patience
to listen
anymore. You need
for me to leave,
not speak,
or listen either,

because you have
nothing more to say.

The rain has slowed
to a light mist, the pools of water
on the sidewalk disperse
into the cracks and
concave crevices
of the concrete. The puddles that remain

quiver in the following breeze.

~Gary McCarty

## Porcelain Truth

I remember coming home to you
and your proclamation of guilt,
determined as you were
to begin with truth.

Your telling me of your night in my absence
with another man who claimed to love you,
and how you lay with him
in his bed clothed
and covered together until the sun rose,
and my fist went through the window shattering your truth,
and you washed my hand, the porcelain sink streaming red,
clockwise toward the open drain,
and you wrapped my hand, pink rising
to the surface of the gauze and
while my hand healed
we had evidence of your honesty, and
the pink stopped appearing, leaving only bright white
until the hand was unwrapped and its scar revealed
to serve as it does still
to remind me of your directness, your truth telling, your
clarity, so I know that
when you left me, telling me your love had lost its color, had
turned white, I know your words came hard,
cleansed your blood,
leaving it red,
flush with oxygen, and my hand

empty

and white.

~Gary McCarty

## Nothing

Does memory
survive
after you abandon your body?

Seek the answer, if it matters, or
read Kierkegaard, or better,

sweep the floor,
dispose
of the remnants found
in your closets and refrigerator, dress neatly, bathe regularly,

be organized.

Best to leave the questions behind,

for nothing will change
when you leave.  Family may weep, or question or wonder,

but none of these cries,

nothing,

will fall on your ears.

Our lives are scheduled
to collide with time.

~Gary McCarty

## Between Haircuts

Mannequins are wheeled from department store windows,
undressed and dismembered in back rooms,
beige body parts discarded with Christmas trees
stripped of their lights like scaleless fish.
Buses fill and empty.
The man beside me on the Number 3 is no longer there.
My heart beats 6.8 million times.
The cells of my body die and regenerate
in familiar patterns. I am the Ship of Theseus:
exactly the same, yet somehow different.
The moon, after two full cycles, softens
and expands over the city hospital
where the parents of a girl in the burn unit
learn she will not recover.
Doors open and close.
Hands are washed, dried, poured into gloves.
Exams conducted. Taxes paid.
At the concert hall, the conductor lifts her baton.
Giant green melons are unboxed, rolled, skinned, and eaten, the rinds
thrown to the rats, who chew and shit them out.
Puddles stand and fall.
The earth warms, then cools,
then warms again.
A young man gives up his seat on the Number 3
to a pregnant woman. Two sets of cells divide and multiply
within her; two hearts beat.
In the town where I was born,
the gypsy moths are weaving their fabulous nests.

~Taylor Altman

## My Name is Not Gregor

My name is not Gregor,
A cockroach I am not,
But there are cracked bowls in the sink,
And a broken dish on the mantle.

Voiceless, speechless,
I stand alone in my family's room,
My hard shell burns with wounds,
I am unable to heal them.

A thoroughbred ran while I was asleep,
His rider untrained and unbridled,
Thin legs now unable to catch up,
Shrinking presence like mist in the wind.

It grows dark with the rising sun,
Peonies fading in the garden,
My love will no longer feed me,
And I fear I am all alone

~Joshua Harris

## Walkthrough Inspection

Property Manager—
come on in.

Excuse my large collection of bottles;
it's a menagerie of my own human-ness.
I am only human after all,
and that's maybe all I have.

But look! Beep-beep.
The smoke alarm in the living room is working—
I rushed to twist it back in place.
(We all rip these things out you know,
like illicitly ripping the tag off a mattress,
or lying to someone you just met,
or lying to someone you've known for 6 years
who knows you best;
just a silly harmless thing we all do).

They just won't shut up.

I ripped the one out in my bedroom
so I could smoke in there,
my eyes drooping out the open window
at the cats zigzagging
in shadowy agitation.

The kitchen is in ok shape;
today I ate a radish.
I just wanted that to be out in the open;
there should be no secrets between us.
(The middle of my tongue tastes spicy
in an earthy sort of way.)

You can replace me once I move along
and I will leave this house so empty
it will be as if my thoughts never had a home here.
It will be so beautiful;

so empty of
me.

I want to be a perpetual
cocoon.
Metamorphosis sounds like so much pressure,
but sleeping a lot sounds pleasant.

Have you slept well, recently?

Have you seen the cats?

Property Manager—
have you ever tried a radish?
It will kiss you so hard
you will lose your sense of taste.

~Andrew Rogers

# PART TWO

*"If he loved me—goes the thought—would he still do this?"*

## Los Arcos

A diesel parade of trucks staccato
their brakes at the round-about
where we stand on broken concrete
outside the hostel.

I spit flu down the grate
as the bus rolls in; wait for Anne
and Barb to limp up the steps; then sit,
shivering, in the sun.

Our heads loll as the smooth road
lifts and weaves through hill-fort towns,
sprouting fields and bougainvillea patios;
everything made of stone;
houses, fences, walls, the Way.

Light streams over its crushed surface
edging the highway; the trail
switching back behind a hedge
that tunnels an overpass.

I see Puerto Rico,
head down, forging his faith
through lines of trees. His bright
blue windbreaker flags among the pines;
red and white poles set a fierce pace.

At the bar last night, a hot toddy warming
my hands, he mused that pilgrimage
was not a titanium heart wrapped
in nylon. "Do not be afraid to ride
when clouds come your way, mi amigo.
Take the bus.
There is plenty of road ahead
for all of us."

I looked back, but he is lost
in the scale of a mountain.

~Keith Inman

## Fountain of Renouncement

Soft hills say nothing of Charlemagne's defeat
of Aigolando. Though, the churches do,
their bell towers and giant stork nests.

Fred mentions he is struggling and may leave
the Way. His daughter's ashes weigh-heavy
in his backpack. He wishes for Finis Terra (final earth).

The loose gravel of our steep climb rolls like alleys
under our feet. Fuente Reniega trickles today. "The Devil
wont be tempting to quench our thirst today", I say.

Barb laughs, "Doesn't he know
about aluminum water bottles." Above her,
turbines churn in never ending wind.

We take vista pictures beside a metal cut-out
of Don Quixote charging the yellow canola fields
amassed like troops in the valley
below snow-capped alps.

~Keith Inman

# Among the Core-fired Ashes of Faith

~ Cruz de Ferro

We follow a pebbled road along an untiled
mud-brick wall guarding a red-earth field;
yellow arrows curb the home on the corner;
the trail winding into mountains that smolder
with purple and gold flowering shrubs.

Anne and Fred walk ahead as slate homes
appear, then disappear as we ascend past fonts
of mirrored water reflecting sky; sheep
as landscape to themselves. A dark horse
swishes its tail, nips at flies.

Near the summit, a thin pole rises
from a stockade of waist deep stones ~
if these are offers of sin, then there is more here
then the foundation of any church ~

the girl in front of me places a rock
on a ledge and falls against the fence.
She sobs uncontrollably as the man
at Anne's side collapses. Eyes closed,
prayer spills from his mouth as his friends
try to lift him, but he is liquid.

A shadow detaches from the road; a storm
pushed by wind. Puerto Rico, in black,
climbs the unstable stack, lays a hand
on the staff of the cross, and Wails!
as if the world sears his iron heart.

Fred strolls among the faithful, turning this way
and that, the weight of his daughter's ashes
shed from his shoulders the way a crown
of birds leave a roost. Anne stares as pilgrims

keep coming. Stones, mementoes, added to the cold
furnace of loss. She turns to me, "Can we go?"

The Way winds down and onward, freshly rent
from recent rains that had torn the hillside open.

~Keith Inman

## Los Templarios

~ What makes one brother better than the other:
Ishmael over Isaac, Isaac over Ishmael.


You were first
to go to university.
We drove you there, gave moral support,
but work for father was scarce.
You were on your own. Me,
I stayed home and played sports.

Later,
when father was rarely home building infrastructure
in distant villages, my equipment
was paid for.

But you stayed away,
learning paths
of a new city. Buying
your own equipment.

Today, I wear your gloves
in the cold.

You were a bit smaller than me. So
the palm's are tight as I walk
the long k's of the Camino,
my fingers swelling.

An engineer, you knew
how to design puzzles, while I
an installer, learned
how to fit them together,
how to make them work.

I'm sorry I missed your last call,
your phone bill listing

that you'd punched an 8
instead of a 5,

before staring at the night, your eyes
turning to glass.

Perhaps,
you wanted to tell me
how cancer works

so I would know.

~Keith Inman

## The Weave of Heaven

A chain-mailed Anne poses
beside a red ensign'd Templar
in full regalia, a leashed hawk
on his forearm.

They do a selfie.
He swipes her credit card
on his cell phone,
loads the file and sends.

Herring bone clouds roof our climb
between wire fencing entwined
with wooden crosses; the path ending
at a guttered street with beamed houses.

Our raw selves gather in a small
romanesque church; sections of ceiling
repaired with steel mesh and plaster.

There are not enough monks for vespers.
So a whisper of faithful join the choir. One
is a women. Her green and red jacket oreo'd
between brown sacrament.

Their voices resound as they stand,
sit, stand and sit through a ringing harmony
of stone echoes that eventually drains
to silence.

Many in the pews clasp their hands
resisting the urge to applaud.

"Imagine," Anne muses as we cross
the street on our way to supper,
her arms locked in front of her.

"A women singing Gregorian Chant
in church. And heaven didn't fall."

~Keith Inman

## My Movie of Prokofiev

In my movie of Prokofiev, he sings
and cavorts. I know, he was caustic and reserved.
Nevertheless, the music transforms him
into a wolf with a fife to its lips, into
Romeo trying on Juliet's gown, to feel
the shimmering moonlight on his skin.

These transfigurations boil Stalin's brain
as he reviews the high-stepping, great-coated
army. Through his grave eyes he sees Prokofiev
marching, a rifle aching his womanly flesh.
Prokofiev's leapfrogging notes grate his ears.
What do these musical hi-jinks contribute
to the Soviet of oilcans and wrenches?

Secretly, Stalin plays Lieutenant Kije at night
to make the little man strut. But the little man,
like a Trotskyite, rebels. Now Stalin
has a grudge. Not only is the so-called music
disrespectful to the sanctity of labor,
but it seriously flops in his garish boudoir.
He rips up his program of Romeo and Juliet
and sprinkles it on the composer's photo.

In my movie of Prokofiev, the music
cannot be contained by fingertips on keys.
It somersaults and trampolines over rooftops
becoming what it wants—elf, ballerina, forest.
Stalin, harrumphing, peeks through the leaves,
choking on each mossy note. "Endless,"
he says in sleep, "I don't like things
without ends." He sends Prokofiev's wife away.

No matter how sad Prokofiev becomes,
the music whistles through Moscow streets.
It never stops toying with the workers' hearts,

befuddling them. They lay down their pliers
to listen. They sigh. They grin. They knock off
early to have vodka and sex with the wife.
They don't stress about making the little guy strut.
They erect a statue to their hero, Prokofiev,
where he sits until this day, under the fiery petals
of cherry blossoms. He appears to be blushing.

~Mark Gordon

## Jiving with The Wind

I have to admit that I went a little crazy
after my husband died.

I was seventy, afraid that I'd go into a tailspin
down that whirlpool of despair
that I've gone down before
even when Lionel the Labrador Retriever
ate his last kibble.

It's dark down there. Something like a basement
with all the lights out. It's dank.
What's worse, it's hard to get out.

It's like trying to climb up a greasy wall,
only to slip again, fall back, getting
weaker, less confident with each feeble attempt.

Then someone dared me to zipline
across a gulley, at least a hundred feet
in the air. What got into me?
I have no idea. I've always been
a little edgy when it came to heights.

But there I was, a hundred feet up,
this old wrinkled lady, with all my friends
from Zumba class, taking pictures on their Cells.

I can't say for sure that the trip across that gulch
saved me from depression. But it sure
took me into another realm. How can I describe it?
Kind of like jiving with the wind.

And I know my husband was somewhere
between the leaves on an oak tree
I saw zipping down, and sunlight, applauding.

~Mark Gordon

## A Capitol March

They were handing out these necklaces,
The shiny cheap beaded ones of different colors,
The ones I twist and twist and sometimes untwist—
I'd taken three that day:
Green must have been for a "familiar struggle,"
Orange for a "self-struggle,"
Purple for the "struggle" of a friend.

So suicide is euphemized.

A group of us had gathered to hear some lady speak.
It was strange that I'd never known her before—
She seemed to think we had a lot in common.
I can't remember exactly what she said,
Something about 13.7 seconds:
How often someone "commits."
To commit to something . . .
As if it doesn't take mere seconds—a whim.

Thoughts of that girl, that sister
Raced into my mind, as always
Whenever I see blood, scars,
Whenever I hear "suicide" or even simply "death."
But I stayed standing till I felt a tickle on my jaw.

I sat down on a tree's uncomfortable roots,
With my trophies around my neck.
And I waited.
Once I'd waited long enough on that rough bark,
That uneven ground, covered with those itchy needles,
Needles that could make you scratch and scratch,
I stood and I brushed them off,
I thanked the volunteers
For being, I guess,
I got on my bike,
I rode to my house,

And I wondered where my sister was.
Then I wondered if she was still alive,
And I wondered if I'd see her again.
I couldn't cry.

~Gabriela Alvarado

## Bitter

I feel nasty inside—slimy
with tar oozing through my guts
past my roadkill heart
when I hear my family talk about
how perfectly-timed his death was;
how beautifully God orchestrated
those final days,
that he was able to officiate my sister's weddings
able to spend one last day with the family
able to pass
without pain in the end—
I feel nasty inside
when my family talks about his
beautiful death
because I wish I could appreciate it—
but I'm too busy
feeling the emptiness of my birthday
four days later
and wishing he'd made it
to my graduation
the following month.

~Cailey Blair

## The Waiting Room

A room with well-thumbed magazines:
*Time* with a global warming penguin

Women's magazines on how to feel
OK eating foods you shouldn't have

A religion magazine cover with
question marks

That children's magazine with hidden
pictures

One side of the waiting room is for
lab patients, the other x-ray

The door leads to a corridor
with many closed rooms

The wall television always has soaps
or talk shows

I fluff my hair trying to make it look
thick—then recalled when I had none

~Carol Smallwood

## Mile Marker 154, Kingman Arizona

She pretends to be asleep
when they cross into California
wheels spelling out what's been
on her mind for the last hundred miles:
*Did he ever really love me?*
Rubber breathes into asphalt
stretching itself to fill the gaps in her memory
threads connect all the moments when she thought
she was happy to the stomach pains she
could not place.

*If he loved me*
–goes the thought–
*would he still do this?*
And while this used to mean how he complained
about her tiny habits he used to love
or the time he made fun of her cooking
right to the neighbor's face
or the blank stare he gets when he
stays up too late.
No, today *this* means rousing her
too early to drive across state lines
on a trip she didn't ask for
and then refusing to talk to her
static of the radio her only companion
as they put the sun to their backs
drive as fast as the car will go.

He doesn't hear the tires sighing
into a road beyond repair.
Instead he's all metal on bone
scraping loud enough
to block out the thoughts
she can sleep off
but he can only try to outrun.

~Bella Pori

## Frank

I bring you tea light candles of humility
so beside the point, they echo
their own smoky darkness.
I bring you temperance.
Temperance like a garden gnome out front,
or small succulents, potted and pebbled in ironic plastic tubs.
And in return, you show me the fanatic part of town,
a wrecked glory, an older, post-new thrashing you.
In return, you bring me the corpse of your happy youth
zipped up in a body bag too big for a child so small.

Here we are, temperate, fanatic,
a barely locked door wind-battered into song
and at least we're both frank.
Together we bemoan the precious sins of our fathers
and mothers and friends and lovers and whatever we haven't lost yet.
Because somebody always croaks, and you'll tell a joke and I'll cry
and at least we'll both be frank
— you can only ever be Frank
An embattled myth,
and that's all.

~Charika Swanepoel

# Love, Like a Skull

## 1. Young Love

I had a myth once,
a wonderful enigmatic man
with eyes, blue as Shiva's skin,
arms like minarets and a mind
mad as many a wrathful god's.
Though his word was law and
His reign sublime —utterly,
my myth was flawed and full
of loopholes and lumps and lies.
Not only this, but all men die.

## 2. Revelation Love

Will you collapse at my funeral,
red and wet with loss?
Will you die with me, evoke me
like the gospel every night before bed?
Will you want another revelation,
more tongued flames and haloed love?
Will I have burnt your Paris down
black and cratered with loss?
Will you die with me, love
when all our holiness is spent?

## 3. Relentless Love

you never leave, love,
nothing about you
ever leaves,
I can feel you gazing
from the bottom of the ocean
where your eyes lay, scattered pebbles.

If ever Death sends you back, my blue-eyed boy,
meet me at Galilee, where nothing ever leaves
and we'll crown ourselves with the humility of our loss
and we'll waltz about the waves like martyrs slain
and we'll be as we were, relentless, in love, insatiable.
if ever Death sends you back, my ocean-eyed love.

~Charika Swanepoel

## 78th Avenue & Woodhaven Boulevard, Queens

Film cartridges of your first wedding collect dust
In the cabinet of the basement we live in now

Forty-three years frozen in time below your
Adopted parent's tutelage & you still come in

Late on Tuesday nights piss drunk from the Irish
Bar in the neighborhood where you say you feel

The most like yourself & the most unlike
The things your wife expected of you & in

Those dreary nights you send me messages
Via airwaves about how glad you are that I

Kissed you & how happy you are when I call
Sitting on that same barstool decades at a time

Your son graduates grade schools one at a time
Wearing flat caps & tassels & getting hugged

By all of us who love him & cheer for him &
Hold his head up while he cries on the E Train

Coming home to Queens we rock in the empty car
Held like the two children we are in the forward sway

I sing to him softly & say the kinds of prayers I
Wish they had said for me, I say them to him &

At Forest Hills we depart the train coming home to
An empty house, you waiting for no one at the corner bar.

~Sara Marron

## Skeleton

**1.**

There's a skeleton in my living room.
My mother bought it for when
holiday season comes 'round,

but it's been there for longer
than last February, when I learned
that even St. Valentine was celibate.

My mother said that she equates it
to a death in the family, I guess
that explains the plastic body.

**2.**

I can see those unmoving eyeholes,
letting me know that this is permanent.
That I will have to learn to live with it.

So, I packed my bags and left to go back
to school, and I built a two thousand,
six-hundred-mile wall against it.

But I came home drunk one night,
tripped toward my bed and balled
my naked fists at its toothy smirk.

**3.**

Right now, I'm staring at a girl,
whose beauty is so elegant that
I wish for nothing more than to talk.

I got my eyes checked, but I swore
it clicked its calcium-deficient feet

down the hallway, and clunked

its tailbone next to hers. I needed to
tell her that it's sitting by her side, that
I hope everything will be alright.

4.

What I wanted to say is that
I was devastated when my father
said that word — "divorce."

But I nodded my head,
let my brother speak for me
and quietly filled out paperwork.
    (for my latest speeding ticket)

My sister cried and ran to her boyfriend.
My brother cursed and called his girlfriend.
I sat there at the table, filling out a form.

~Alex Stanley

## Atmospheric Depressions

**1.**

A weather map of the North Pacific
is a string of storms
marching east
from Japan, along Kamchatka,
riding the Aleutian chain to
crash into North America.
Once I was planning for a crossing of the
Gulf of Alaska—small tug, big tow— so I
sought a meteorologist in Valdez. He
showed me storms and the measured lows
in the center: 989, 983, 995. He told me the
interval between these atmospheric depressions:
36 hours. 18 hours. A break of two days.
He was more accurate than
I thought a weatherman could be. They
have satellites, he explained, to see the
depressions coming. "We track them. Watch
them fill in. Time and enough wind reduces
a storm at sea to just a shower."

**2.**

Depression, you told me, is anger
turned inward. You were furious
as you said this.
I didn't want to talk about it.
Your anger is the loud kind; I have
never been called an "asshole" before by
someone I loved.
Mine is a slow simmer
which erupts, an explosion in an overheated
room. At least that's how I see it.

This is the ugly inheritance from my father.
He fought with me and my brothers,

yelling and stomping and open-handed blows.
It was a winter farm, no place to hide.
It was a barn strung with accusations, a childhood
that Dickens would have understood.

3.

Last time all my brothers go together
it was to bury the old man. I looked
at the five of us—three dark, two fair.
Same eyes, puppies from different
litters, alike enough to amuse the wives.
Wild Bill, drunk.
Fair second one wisecracking with a
practiced skill, teasing until it hurts, my favorite brother.
Yet he also got the temper, slamming car doors
until a window breaks, walking off more good jobs
than most men will hear off.
Fair Keith and silent Verne, a slow fuse and slower to forget.
Verne took three years of a classmate's
teasing and answered,
at last, with the classmate in the hospital.
Traction. Reaction.

My brothers and I in a loose circle while a
hired preacher said some words.
Took turns at the shovels,
not much said. Lift and push,
toss and scatter.
Dirt falling into a grave like thunder.
In turns we watch it fill, wait
for some shower of late
forgiveness.

~Travis Stephens

# PART THREE

*"We consume darkness in loss,
ingesting eclipses."*

## As We Go

When the oaks topple like the elms,
when the ash and beech,
weakened by heat and drought,
succumb to insects or disease,
when the tall canopy is gone
and white pines and spruce
are like dead Christmas trees;
when the dirt blows away,

our children's children
can go to the Brooklyn Botanic Garden
where twelve years ago,
curators began installing
drip irrigation
to transplant a history
of postage-stamp habitats:
New Jersey pine barrens,
wetlands, kettle ponds,
limestone cliffs.

Perhaps some creatures
will make their way there—
newts, iridescent darning needles.
Perhaps our children's children
will hear the calls of birds and frogs.
They will say *oh the wind*
*stirring the reeds*
*makes a small music.*

~Cathie Desjardins

## I Rode a Tortoise

I rode a tortoise at the San Diego zoo.
I was three – my earliest memory.
I waited in the long line on my Daddy's shoulders.
I watched other fathers release their children
to a turtle's care.
Then it was my turn.

I laid on my belly.
I grasped the shell's ancient edge.
I laughed loudly.
I rode boldly.
Excited and frightened and fulfilled.

I wonder how that experience shaped me
and why it is the first thing I remember.

I visited the San Diego zoo
forty years later.
Children may not ride tortoises now.
It is a liability issue
and a conservationist issue.
And no "good parent" would ever
do that today.

It saddens me to think that
forty years from now,
no men will remember
riding turtles.

~Rick Jordan

## Delta Journal

**1.**

abandoned bridge
    its surface
sprawled with blue morning glory

**2.**

lonely fall
    in the roadside fields
a ragged scarecrow

**3.**

muggy noon
    dragonflies
darting on highway hit my windshield

**4.**

autumn equinox—
    a three-legged dog
stands at the crossroads

~Jianqing Zheng

## Aylan Kurdi

What does it taste like
To rebuild
After
    War?

Is there a moment
when one remembers
how the
    churches
used to look
how the
                           flowers
used to smell
how the
        breeze
used to feel?

is that moment
                      tart
        like cherries picked too soon before harvest?
does it ache
like knowing
your neighbor is dead?

I wonder
just how we
plant seeds
after they've ground the dirt so fine,
that even the fruits are made of bone

~Rhea Ranno

## Abandoned

stepping from the tree break
the rabbit slung over my shoulder
head down tethered by withered sinew
one red pearl adorning its winter white ruff

a harvested cornfield before me barren to disuse
the shorn stalks now bone shards cracking underfoot
the abandoned house beyond it
paint mottled like age spots sun singed frost blistered

I studied the shack
a skull with vortex windows darkened
the door a splintered maw
wooden slats jagged as gnawed teeth

a cold wind moaned through the marrowless bones
scattering the shed's memories across the broken field

~Steve Gerson

## Ingesting Eclipses

**1.**

We consume darkness in loss, ingesting eclipses.
When earth and moon fail to syncopate, our axis askew,
Truth becomes dross. Even gilding fails to validate.

**2.**

Heat-steeped cement, iridescent, turns vapor to flame.
A leaf on the ground colors Fall, mocking with vibrancy.
Mirages fail to satiate, quenching with aridity.

**3.**

There's no reckoning a mind's cyclonic confusion.
Though we assume, destiny downdrafts in rotating winds.
Clouds move north and south; cicadas siren suffering.

~Steve Gerson

## Was

through the door
the bed

once with two warm furrows
is wintered

covers tightly sealed
comforter creaseless as ice

pillows aligned at right angles
shuttered like boards squared

I sleep in another room
now

~Steve Gerson

## All That Summer

All that summer my mother shucked
sweet corn on the porch,

and sometimes silk got caught
in her wedding ring,

and sometimes I passed to retrieve
a baseball disappeared

under Bob Castanero's 1959 Chevrolet.
All that summer I died

between Natalie's Maxwell's breasts,
unaware of the story inside

the story of what happens in a town
where one is small and cannot

know what passes in the night, the gravel,
the figures in the window

drinking beer and watching Jeopardy!
and flicking their thumbs

at moths—all the flesh-colored moths
that never came to me.

~Carl Boon

## The Catholic in Istanbul

It's very hot at 4 a.m. and the city
is strange

and I'm strange inside it, thinking
of the nothing

that precedes a life and what's
just after—

a cup of coffee, two men moving
toward the Bosphorus.

A dog begins to bark on this street
they call Joker Street,

a fantasy, a failed garden. No one
laughs at me now.

I curl inside the heat and cross
my arms—

no one prays if no one's there
to listen.

I remember my mother telling me
St. Nicholas came here

once in the cold, was hungry,
was fire,

was turned away. He walked south
toward the Marmara Sea

and was turned away again. Tomorrow
I'll drink a beer

at the Last Ship Cafe and tell the waiter
how doomed we are.

~Carl Boon

## Downtime

In the park
near my home
there are numerous pigeons
and just enough
hawks.
Once, I watched
as a red-tailed bolt
shot like a dragon's tongue
on an unsuspecting squab.
An explosion of feathers--
swirling, tumbling, cavorting
and mingling; cascading
over the landscape, leaving
vacant air.

My father often said
in this life,
you will be one
or the other,
predator
or prey, the tearer
or the torn.
So by all means
be the hawk,
be THE HAWK,
BE THE HAWK.

But I always thought,
given a choice,
I'd much prefer

to be the feathers.

~John Jay Speredakos

## I Want to Ask My Mother

I want to ask my mother
what exactly my father did
what happened all those years ago

but it will only make her cry
if not at first soon after
does she need another reason

I resort to sorting her jewelry drawer
for the twenty billionth time
untangling sparkly tumbleweeds

remembering what made Dad laugh
what brought him to tears at night
his silhouette at our kitchen table

chain smoke stroking his hair back
I only know he was sent here     there
wherever they send cracked cameos

and if ever there was one
it is hard to imagine individuals
stay in one box for life

I want to ask my mother
but does it matter now
when her mind is on her own flesh

sinking in the palms of her hands
the curve of her pageant-winning neck
I ask if she still needs this key chain

two heart-shaped red-leather cutouts
baseball stitched together at the edges
"Dad made that" she asserts

reminding me of the popsicle stick box
he once wrapped for me
embarrassed yet proud

he made it while recovering    here
there    I filled it years ago
with a few small pieces I gathered

~Maria Sebastian

## Little Girls and Alligators

The irony of course,
was we were in the Peace River.
Florida's Peace River, which has
doubtless witnessed turmoil
enough; brutality, savagery, pain
enough, to give its meander
pause. Just ask its bones.
The ones staring back
from the black and peaty water.
The ones we came to find.
And you WERE dead, certainly.
Dead and partially devoured.
There's that.
Even now your tail was half missing,
your face the target of turkey vultures
with their own red needs.
I called to my daughter in shock.
We stared at your swollen, bloated
white-bellied carcass.
There wasn't much discussion,
there needn't be.
She asked the obvious;
I answered the only
way I could.

And so, not with a knife
but a spade, a sharpened shovel
better built for burying,
I began. And I even
pitied the Irish Rovers
for providing me
with the only tune
I had available
for such occasions:
"A long time ago
when the Earth was green..."

I slid some slate
behind your toe
for better resistance.
*"there were more kinds of animals*
*than you've ever seen..."*
I cut down through the scutes,
the impossibly glossy
ancient armor.
*"They'd run around free*
*while the Earth was bein' born..."*
Through the tendons,
the fiber
*"and the loveliest of them all*
*was the Unicorn."*
and finally, *"Well there were*
*green alligators..."*
bone.

And I was sorry. Truly.
Sorry about the dinosaurs.
Sorry about the asteroid
that deprived you and your kin
of another few eons
of quadrupedal supremacy.
Sorry for the handbags
the boots the belts the wallets.
Sorry for the bad rep
with the whole Captain Hook thing
(though I know that was a crocodile),
and sorry about the confusion.
Sorry we conquer our fears
by taking trophies.
Sorry for it all...
But you're just
so beautiful.
So.
And not built for it,
but rather; to slide silently
under a belly,
twisting, rolling, gorging,

dismembering
limb by limb
till all that remains
is stain and memory.
As beautiful
as my daughter's shining eyes.

But know this, gator:
I did it out of love for her,
not hatred for you.
Not fear, not vengeance,
not sport, not rage, not greed.
None of the vices we invented
and at which we so excel.
Instead, back home, there was
"Wow, Calliope, is it real?
Can I touch it? So cool.
Did you find it or cut it off?
Really? Disgusting! And
so cool."

So... you'll be remembered, alligator.
Not that you'd care; but it's something
we seem to want very much
on our side of the pond.
You'll be remembered
in hearts, minds, imaginations,
dreams and nightmares.
In show-and-tell and sleep-overs.
In the whispers of childhood
and my daughter's toothy smile.
When the new turkey vultures
open their needy beaks--
and the Peace, as ever,
runs red--

one way or another
you will be
remembered.

~John Jay Speredakos

## To the Tarot Card Reader at the Kit Kat Club

I was out of place at a bar that offered nightly drag revue shows,
And sold $13 martinis with plastic figurines or lollipops floating in them.

But the drag show was over now, and you pollinated from table to table
With an offer or request that the other diners dismissed with a tight smile.

You were at the tail end of your thirties but your eyes looked older;
Somehow, even your gold ringlets and unfussy white dress looked tired.

When you landed at our table, you laid out your offer like the starter bread:
Tarot card readings. That table in the corner. Fifteen dollars. Credit cards okay.

Out of the corner of my eye, I saw your table, empty
Except for the cards and a lace doily, encircled in the glow of a single candle.

I tried to meet my friends' eyes and enjoy my steak frites,
But I wondered when someone would sit down across from you.

You wondered it too, though you sat with a patient crossed-leg
And glanced around casually, careful not to look at anyone for too long.

You squared the edges of your card deck over and over,
Picked invisible lint from the doily, and studied the flicker of the candle.

Before long, I—committed skeptic—could almost not resist
The urge to cross the dim bar, take the empty chair, and plunk my money down.

I was suddenly very interested in fates and futures,
Not so much mine, but yours.

~Chad Baker

## Vagabond Soul

The eastern sun
washed away my evening pleasures.
I put away the pipe,
I clean up my face.
Still, the mirror is blackened.

Eyes that strain to see colors,
What is the meaning of remedy?
I misplaced my chaos,
I misplaced my exquisite hatred,
and destroyed my will to fix my own problems.

Dry lips covering an aging tongue,
a vagabond soul wishing to be loved.
Abnormalities, I am surrounded.
Disasters, I am dumbfounded.
I am walking through this dark sky alone.

Peeling back the fingers,
waiting for the sting of remembrance.
Sadness, I know you.
Insanity, I need you.
My own twisted adolescence,
that I lived by the definition.

~Tabatha Jenkins

## Shards

You smelled like
the roses you always placed
on my bedside table.
Only this time you didn't deserve
the delicate touch
of my admiring hand.
Because there was nothing left
to admire.

I never wanted to
again let you feel
the security of my love.
Your words were still as sharp
as the shards of glass
remaining from your grandmother's
broken, antique vase.

You didn't believe I would break it.
Just like I didn't believe
you'd break me.

~Tabatha Jenkins

## Maybe It's Just Me

I am alone in a room with no windows, knotted wood floors. There's a clock, relentless, keeping track of all the minutes I've wasted. No one comes to the door—if there even is a door—and no one calls my name.

The sky is so very dark but it's sunlight that frightens me most.

~Erin Jamieson

# PART FOUR

*"Don't look can mean look at what you didn't see in the first place."*

## Hindsight

My love was an ocean
    I should have drowned you in

~Edythe Rodriguez

## Fajardo

sun-warmed tides greet
me at the shoreline,

A toe.

Another.

children run past unabashed,
dive headfirst into
glassy blue birthright.

"Cálmate, mija"
She whispers, whisking
foam slippers onto my feet.
She cradles me in her current,
her salt skin robe and I chuckle,

remembering how my big
toe tapped the water,
at my production,
my uncomfortable shudders,

at how I've been living
afraid of my own mother

~Edythe Rodriguez

## Prostitute: San Francisco

The back seat of the grimy taxi
my mother herded me into
when I was twelve, when remembered,
can still summon the smell
of a pack of chain-smoking hacks
choking on the same stale jokes.
*Don't look* can mean look
at what you didn't see in the first place.
The woman's brash cocktail dress,
red velour, looked like someone lashed
a tacky theater curtain
around the burlesque act of her body.
Ruin rouged her face, a harried
portrait of a Punchinello
smeared by the hand of an angry child.
Sidewalk sloped under her heels
of glossy black magic, making one leg
longer than the other, so now
I see her as a sex compass, carving
graceful circles into frozen lives,
or one of those folklore mountain goats
from Italy or the Swiss Alps,
caught only when hounded
to level ground where, hapless,
they scamper around, hunted where
anything virgin can no longer astound.
If we say *Don't love* will we love
what we haven't seen? To that younger me
I can still say, and sometimes do,
You don't need to sell yourself
for streets of sadness. In the fanfaronade
of night traffic, the baroque flames
blooming from hissing grills
in Japanese restaurants, you can still send
the golden earthquake drumming
beneath buildings of blind fog,
through the slums of slack heartbeats,

and from the back seat of loss
arrive in the city of lights to find
your pure self still waiting to leave.

~Matthew James Babcock

## Metamorphosis

Ascending in rhythmic fabulation
as we consumed heady leaves of
life eternal.

Elongating while shedding layers
as we came in and then slipped out,
wrapping ourselves in velveteen blankets,
spinning ceaselessly into a freeing frenzy.

Would we be an amorphous mess,
with one wrong step to the left, or to the right,
a bit off balance on a luminous night?

Would I be nothing but a 'pillar
of tiny wings trapped in human form,
disintegrating slowly, never to achieve
a higher state?

They say it takes about 50,000 cells
to turn into a butterfly.
You do realize, you found me at 50.

~Effie Pasagiannis

# If We Could Only Slow It Down

~ A Villanelle


If we could only slow it down
we could dissect the moment into halves
head to the skies like deer, arms to the ground

We could break apart the mortar's sound
all to a full stop living off-script,
if we could only slow it down

Who will be taking off his own crown?
Let's be done with the vestiges of time,
head to the skies like deer, arms to the ground

To breathe as if we are no longer bound
by two masters, we thought we had a choice,
if we could only slow it down

Not needing to turn those clocks around
we could release the debts of history,
head to the skies like deer, arms to the ground

Blood no more remains to be found,
red is a color painted on canvas,
if we could only slow it down,
head to the skies like deer, arms to the ground


~Effie Pasagiannis

## Wounds

I dig at old wounds
just to see
if I can feel
the pain
again.
Just to see if I still bleed.
If I still cry.
If I still feel.

~Lora Larivere

## Beauty

I resist love.
Every time I am close.
I ruin it.
I get right to edge and then stop.
Same can be said for my orgasms.
The irony is not lost on me.

~Lora Larivere

## The Edge

We romanticize the memories
because
who wants to relive the sadness?
Who wants to look back and think
and feel
and be
the worst parts?
We want to be the best.
Even better.
The romantic,
the heart felt
moments that perhaps never actually were.
Memories that are the happiest,
are the moments we never had.

~Lora Larivere

## Moments and Mundane

We talk about our day.
The mundane
The boring.
The busy.
Peppered with sexual desires.
Fantasies we will later live out.
If only for a few minutes,
I am aroused by the idea
that I make you hard.
And then we return to discussing
the boring.
The busy.
The mundane.

~Lora Larivere

## Wild Air

I needed it all my life, wind gripping lungs, open mouth for hard
disintegrating storms, chest puffed-out, a harmless night
of touch-me-there where it throbs, stomach up, need me less
breathe-in, breathe-out, a tasteless poison, a white scar on the horizon
sunset punishment or chaotic inhalations of a nightmare
in the back of the truck, predatory coyotes, asshole-wolves
my angry aunts, my doped-out uncle, a scattered purple night.

~Mateo Lara

# Destruction as the Cause of Coming into Being

~ after Edward Hopper's "Summer Evening"

I let him fuck me
behind the cherry tree
because anything
is better than
being bored.

Pink makes me sick
so that's why
I wear it.

Give it to me.
I'm asking for it.

We do it in the dark only
because it makes him
forget I have parts
that break.

I stick pins in my skin
1, 2, 3, until
my brain makes
constellations.

When I kissed him
I saw my body rotting
in the ditch behind
his house.

I think he's trying
to say sorry
but all I hear
are the screams
of cicadas.
I once stepped

on a husk, felt
the shell crack
in every bone
of my body.

I, too, long
to become
part of the concrete.

One day my face
will cover magazines—
dead or alive.
You choose.

~Grace McGovern

## The Day Before We Left You

My eyes are green because
of you. Their hushpuppy

droop and wheat blonde
lashes scream father but I

would give it all up for that
green. You taught me to wear

lavender so they look freshly
watered. But yours are faraway

nowadays, set on autopilot–
watering can, sewing machine,

bible, watering can, sewing machine,
bible. Pieces of a life dashed,

a glass vase from shaky hands.
At least the flower cannot shatter,

cannot lodge itself beneath
the skin. Today, you call me

by my name. I hold your hand
and, oh, it feels like mine.

~Grace McGovern

87

# When the Bank Says My Account Was Drained

by someone from Louisiana, when they tell me
all of the hundreds of hours worked at three jobs was
$50 here, $200 there just stolen away over a series
of weeks, money saved for my move to Boston for grad school,

when they ask do I know anyone from that area,
I think back to the night you drove to my freshman dorm
because it was my first night away, and you knew I was scared,
that I was also terrible at making new friends, so you came

to save me and get me invites to college parties, but especially
I think about how by 8 o'clock we were both starved since
I hadn't thought to bring any food for the fridge, which led
to us driving around my new town in search of groceries,

then giving up and pulling in to this gas station with no name
and expired cans of Vienna sausage, where I spent my only dollars
on bags of Fire Hot Cheetos, meaning we had to drive to campus to steal
toilet paper from the rec center, and we laughed so hard stuffing it

in our purses because this was our first ridiculous act as adults,
and by the time we got back, so much night had gone by
we just crashed into the bed that was too small for even me,
with happy, orange-stained fingertips, so, now, please tell me—

how do I explain any of this to the woman on the phone?
The answer is I can't, so instead I tell her there is no one.
She tells me I need to come in to make a claim. And weeks later
when you text asking when you can come visit me in Boston,

I say maybe next month. It'll just be like old times

~Bryanna Licciardi

## I Survived #METOO

The wolf's no longer at my door
I've had no lawyers call
The ones I so innocently
(I swear)
flirted with
had a drink with
made mutual,
consensual
(I swear)
contact with
those many years ago
have made no attempts
to contact me

Yet...

I thank god,
I'm not famous
Enough!
rich
Enough!
Nor in the public eye
Enough!
I'm no Harvey, Kevin, Bill or Brett

Below the radar I fly
A stealthy wraith
my invisible shield,
my absence of celebrity
keeps me safe

Yet...

I was there
As was she
And just for now

I may seemingly be
beyond her periphery
but doubtless...
not her memory

Don't judge me
Admit it
You were complicit
You wore the skimpy dress
laughed at my jokes
acted impressed
feigned interest
danced with me slow
drank the liquor (I paid for)
Now we both know

Payback's a bitch.

Where's your video?
Where's your proof?
Where's your witness?

Where's the truth?

Stay low
Lay low
This too shall pass
The shadow crossing the window
The creeping death
The Spanish Inquisition
The witches hunt
The Holocaust...
it all ends
eventually

Yet...

I too remember
Her voice
Her words

The force
My urge
The violent surge
Her muffled cry

It's quiet now.

Yet...

Each time the phone rings
I die

~Rollin Jewett

## And After the Accident

~ One man would say to another
Don't move her, she might be bleeding internally


what they didn't say /cause they didn't know /is that the lifeless body /was a long-distance runner /and it preferred coffee to tea /read poems over scrambled eggs /never danced cause it thought it couldn't /skipped meals cause it thought it was growing fatter /refused to join the choir /was afraid of making new friends /kept old ones at arm's length /planted wildflowers /was proclaimed barren /stabbed twice /by the same man it refused to divorce /and was on its way to tell him/ it has a body growing inside

~Ogunkoya Samuel

## The Cousins

We came together infrequently but intensely, with the tenderness of lovers, and the jealousy of thieves.

We knew everything about one another, and nothing at all.

We chased fireflies in August, plucked raspberries that burst in our mouths. We ate snow in December, the Florida cousins' eyes wide as the pale ice melted on their tongues.

We ran inside for a winter meal, the New Jersey chill still on our cheeks, our fingers frozen. We smelled the oysters in the red broth and pulled away, disgusted.

We watched the baby Florida cousin suck her long spaghetti noodles in and out or her tiny mouth. We giggled when the red wine spilled like flower petals on the rug, but hid when the Italian Uncle saw it too.

We shared beds, pillows and tank tops.

We heard them fighting, kept the pillow over the baby cousin's ears. We knew the sound of our Aunt's ribs breaking.

We ate picnics on the beach, the Uncles tossing children in the air between beers. We grilled hotdogs on an open fire and crushed a beer can with our bare feet.

We did not lose the baby. We knew she was swimming.

We should have watched more carefully. We thought she could swim. We wiped her crying face, and felt the precariousness of our position, the fragility of life, the lack of adult attention.

We invented games with live bugs in Nanna's bath tub, chased the greasy dog around the kitchen, peered warily into the darkness of the basement, where the one-eyed angry cat awaited us.

We feared our Grandmother, her lipstick a bright red gash across her face, her eyes eagle-sharp, her hands long talons. We listened to the gossip from under the kitchen table, the grime from the floor marking our dresses. We rubbed the bruises from Grandma's pinch.

We watched the addictions appear, like unwanted guests. The curl of smoke above the Christmas turkey, the rattle of ice splashed with Scotch. The crack vials broken in the bathroom; picking shards of glass from our toes. The weed on the window sill, the cocaine wrapped in tin-foil in his pockets.

We were red-haired, blonde, dark-haired beauties. We were olive skinned, fair, gypsies and princesses. We could have been anyone's children, not family. We shared only memories.

We weren't sure who the actual fathers were, or whether some of us were found, not born into the chaos.

We knew some babies had been given away.

We learned to say leukemia, moved the tubes from our Uncle's IV out of the way and climbed on the couch to watch T.V. next to him.

We drove to Manhattan to visit the hospital. We carried Jello to his bedside. We hid under the bed when the uncle died. We came out later, to find mother's pills and get her to bed. We held hands at the funeral.

We wondered about the uncles in jail, we ran our fingers over each other's hair and tickled the youngest.

We followed Uncle Joe through the garden, loading our arms with basil and tomatoes, the stems itching our fingers.

We crawled under Nana's car to share a joint, our long limbs sprayed with car oil.

We took money from the Moms' purses, we snuck into drive-in movies, we lied about our age or drank the gin from the bottom of the Aunt's glasses.

We took communion and kicked our brothers gently as they went up the aisle.

We kissed older boys, we read poetry, we sang every word to the Rolling Stones' songs and thrust our hips.

We pitched a tent in the backyard and talked while the stars moved slowly across the sky. We never told each other what had happened with him. We wondered if the others knew, or didn't. Or remembered.

We cleaned up vomit when our brothers drank too much, we helped the youngest cousins out of their snowsuit. We pulled the tails off Florida lizards and compared our nipples. We cried over Bob Marley.

We played too rough, broke an arm. Broke a leg, stitched a stomach. We were bitten by dogs and passed kidney stones. We had migraines, PMS, depression, pregnancy scares, freckles and nightmares.

We grew despite the odds.

We went to college, to jail, to law school, to rehab. We owned restaurants, cleaned gutters, used needles on our patients, used needles to get high.

We counseled the homeless.

We were the homeless.

We bought houses, jail bonds, maternity clothes and a bus ticket to California. And weed.

We sold houses, data systems, hamburgers and our bodies. And weed.

We shifted states, memories, agreements, husbands, mental illnesses and values.

We live far away now.

We live in the same town now.

We never see each other. We see each other and reach for one another across the void.

We eat each other up, tenderly. We turn away.

We share holidays, phone calls, a bottle of wine, a joint, old pictures, a few wounds.

We don't share.
We drink too much. We don't drink at all. We should have a drink, sometime.

We remember everything, except the parts no one remembers.

We should have told someone, should have gotten him to stop, should have protected the others.

We should have killed him.

We should forgive him.

We should never forget.

We should move on.

We share stone mosaics, raspberry tarts, old jokes, fading photographs and politics.

We write novels, emails, truths and lies.

We call when things are bad, and we need to know if it is bad for them too.

We call when there's a funny memory.

We don't call at all.

We are the sisters, the cousins, the survivors. We trace our lineage back like the edge of a wave in the sea before it breaks. Here we were, a family, for a moment. Then nothing, molecules dissolved into the wider world.

We blow kisses at the camera in 1978, Christmas lights in the background, snow drifting outside the windows.

We blow up at one another.

We blow smoke into a summer breeze. We watch it drift, and touch our daughters' hair.

We remember the sun on the Florida cousin's baby hair.

We remember the one white Christmas.

We remember the food in the hospital cafeteria, the thirst we felt after smoking our Uncle's weed, the hunger we knew for one another.

We came together infrequently, but intensely, with the tenderness of lovers and the jealousy of thieves.

~Joanell Serra

# CONTRIBUTORS

TAYLOR ALTMAN was born and raised on Long Island and now lives and works as an attorney in San Francisco. She holds a BA from Stanford University, an MFA in creative writing from Boston University, and a JD from Berkeley Law School. Prior to law school, she worked at QuestBridge, an educational non-profit organization, and taught English composition at the College of Southern Nevada. Her work, twice nominated for a Pushcart Prize, has appeared in journals such as Blackbird, Notre Dame Review, and Salamander. Her first collection of poems, Swimming Back, was published by sunnyoutside in 2008.

GABRIELA ALVARADO is a high-school senior in Sacramento, California. She authors the blog, "When Inspiration Strikes," about her poetry-writing process. She spends all the time she can writing and expanding her knowledge of utilizing language.

ALEXIS AVLAMIS's art practice follows in the footsteps of the Surrealist's Automatism. Through improvisation, intuition and by tapping into a stream of consciousness, he organically constructs "landscapes of the mind" aiming at a Cosmic Unity, where human, nature and the artifice co-exist symbiotically.

MATTHEW JAMES BABCOCK, Idahoan, writer, failed break-dancer, an author of Points of Reference (Folded Word), Strange Terrain (Mad Hat), Heterodoxologies (Educe Press), Four Tales of Troubled Love (Harvard Square Editions), and Future Perfect (forthcoming, Engine/Ferry Street Books).

CHAD BAKER graduated from Harvard Law School in 2015 and now works as a legal aid attorney in Chicago. His fiction recently appeared in the journal, From the Depths, and is forthcoming in Ellery Queen Mystery Magazine. Chad's creative nonfiction has appeared in the journal, Lunch Ticket. His plays have been performed at various new play festivals and theater companies in the United States. He is currently a student in DePaul University's Writing and Publishing MA program.

CAILEY BLAIR is a recent college graduate from Cincinnati, Ohio, with a passion for writing and fine art. Her poetry has appeared in several print and online publications, including Weasel Press, Snapdragon: a Journal of Arts & Healing, and The Healing Muse. Additionally, Cailey recently self-published her first poetry chapbook, Stars & Seas. She writes about creative inspiration and art techniques at www.seecaileycolor.com.

CARL BOON lives in Izmir, Turkey, where he teaches courses in American literature at Eylül University. His poems appear in dozens of magazines, including The Maine Review and Posit. A Pushcart Prize and Best of the Net nominee, Boon is currently editing a volume on food in American literature.

CATHIE DESJARDINS is a lifelong teacher, learner and poet. Her writing has been published online in Cognoscenti, and in many newspapers, periodicals and journals. including Pulse and The Christian Science Monitor. Her first book of poems is With Child, (Tasora Press, 2008) and her second book of poems, Buddha in the Garden, will be published in early 2019. She is the current Poet Laureate of Arlington MA.

STEVE GERSON, an emeritus English professor, writes poetry about life's dissonance and dynamism. He's proud to have published in Panoplyzine (winning an Editor's Choice award), The Hungry Chimera, Toe Good, The Write Launch, and Ink & Voices.

MARK GORDON is a novelist and poet who grew up in Halifax, Nova Scotia. His poetry has appeared in numerous literary journals in Canada and the United States, including Poet Lore, Quiddity International and Roanoke Review. His three published novels are The Kanner Aliyah, Head of the Harbour and The Snail's Castle. He is presently living in Toronto, Canada. He maintains the website markgordonauthor.com, which he cordially invites you to visit.

JOSHUA AH HARRIS holds a B.A. from Brown University, a J.D. from UC Davis, and an M.A. in English from San Francisco State University, where he is also currently pursuing an M.F.A. in Creative Writing.

KEITH INMAN's work has won a handful of awards and grants, and can be found in libraries across North America. He lives in the inland port of Thorold, Ontario, Canada, where ships climb the continent.

ERIN JAMIESON holds an MFA in Creative Writing from Miami University of Ohio. Her writing has been published or is forthcoming in After the Pause, Into the Void, Flash Frontier, Mount Analogue, Blue River, The Airgonaut, Evansville Review, Canary, Shelia-Na-Gig, and Foliate Oak Literary, among others. She currently works as a professional freelance writer and teaches English Composition at UC-Blue Ash.

TABATHA JENKINS graduated from the University of Arkansas at Monticello in May 2017 with a Bachelor of Arts in English/Creative Writing. She has been previously published in Adelaide Literary Magazine, the blog 'Friday Night Specials' by Helen Literary Magazine, The Write Launch Magazine, The Scene & Heard Journal, and The Bookends Review. You can learn more about her at her personal website: tabathajenkins.wixsite.com/tabathajenkins.

ROLLIN JEWETT is an award-winning playwright, screenwriter, singer/songwriter, poet, author and photographer. His screenwriting credits include "Laws of Deception" and "American Vampire". His short stories, poetry and photography have been published in numerous literary magazines and anthologies and his plays have been produced all over the world.

RICK JORDAN lives with his wife, cat, dog and in-laws in Lewisville, NC. It is crowded and happy home. When he is not working or writing, he enjoys his square foot garden, Americana music, and hiking the Blue Ridge Mountains. Recent work of his has appeared in Eno Journal, Poetry South, TWJ Magazine and The Dead Mule School of Southern Literature.

MATEO LARA is from Bakersfield, California. He received his B.A. in English at CSU Bakersfield. He is currently working on his M.F.A. in Poetry at Randolph College in Lynchburg, VA. His poems have been featured in Orpheus, EOAGH, Empty Mirror and The New Engagement. He is an editor for RabidOak online literary journal.

LORA LARIVERE puts words where her feelings were, drawing inspiration from despair, heartbreak and melancholy. Her life is her greatest muse.

JAVED LATOO is a medical practitioner based in the UK. Dr. Latoo writes poetry as a hobby. His poems have been published in literary journals and magazines (both print and online) as well as in anthologies. Dr. Latoo likes to use poetry to explore the philosophy of life, mental health and neuroscience. He likes to write in the language of ordinary people, about their everyday thoughts and ordinary insights.

BRYANNA LICCIARDI has received her MFA in poetry from Emerson College. Her debut chapbook SKIN SPLITTING is out now from Finishing Line Press (August, 2017). She is a Pushcart Prize nominee, and co-curates a local poetry reading series called Poetry in the Boro, founded by the Murfreesboro Poet Laureate. Her work appears in journals such as Poetry Quarterly, BlazeVOX, Northern England Review, Peacock Journal, Adirondack Review and Cleaver Magazine. Check out www.bryannalicciardi.com for more.

SARA MARRON is a writer from New York City currently living in Washington, D.C., studying to become a lawyer. She believes in the power of words in every application, with imagination adjudicating as the great equalizer. Read more of her work here: https://sites.google.com/view/saracmarron/home?authuser=0.

GARY McCARTY's poetry examines the relationships that bind human beings, be they lovers, parents, children or strangers, as well as the deceased. Gary has published poems in three anthologies as well as in several literary magazines. He served as poetry editor of *Lichen*. Originally from Brooklyn, New York, Gary now lives in Niagara Falls, Ontario.

GRACE McGOVERN is a recent graduate of Illinois Wesleyan University. She was the recipient of her University's 2016 and 2018 Academy of American Poets College and University Prize, and received Research Honors for my undergraduate poetic project dealing with her identity as a queer woman. Her work has been published in The Academy of American Poets, OUT/CAST, and Illinois's Best Emerging Poets: An Anthology.

EFFIE PASAGIANNIS is a first generation Greek-American lawyer, writer and curator based in New York City. Effie's poetry has been featured in Snapdragon Journal, the Write Launch, Platform Review, Anti-Heroine Chic Magazine and the inaugural print publication of Pen + Brush. Effie has appeared as a featured poet at the Bowery Poetry Club, Arlo Hotels, The Assemblage and Pen + Brush. She is currently working on a chapbook of villanelles as well as a collection of short stories with female protagonists at a crossroads of choice. One of these short stories was recently featured in the September 2018 issue of The Feminine Collective.

LISA POFF is a grad student and single mom of two children. Writing poetry makes Lisa happy, and she hopes her readers feel a connection in this condition called living. Her poetry has been published in the "I Am Strength" anthology, Alexandria Quarterly, Stories That Need to Be Told, Crosswinds, Ghost City Review, Runcible Spoon, Vita Brevis, and is forthcoming in Headway Lit.

BELLA PORI is a law student and poet in Brooklyn, New York. Her poetry can be found in HCE Review, Alternating Current, and FEELINGS, among others. Her political writing can be found on westwingbestwing.com.

RHEA RANNO is a queer poet, born and raised in Boston. Her writing focuses on the universal suffering found only in personal trauma and transformation.

EDYTHE RODRIGUEZ is a Philly-based poet studying creative writing and Africology at Temple University. Her favorite poets are Sonia Sanchez and Amiri Baraka.

ANDREW ROGERS is a musician and political propagandist from Portland, Oregon. He earned his BA in Philosophy at the University of Oregon, where he focused on Analytic Philosophy and Philosophy of Language. He has been published on Open Arts Forum and in The Tiny Mag and Third Point Press. He is currently learning to read Tarot and to take photographs.

OGUNKOYA SAMUEL is a Nigerian physiotherapist. His poems have been published in Kalahari Review, AfricanWriter and Best New African poets anthology 2017. He writes from Lagos.

MARIA SEBASTIAN is an American singer/songwriter and poet living in Clarence Center, NY. She also teaches public speaking and English in the SUNY system and plans to settle one day in Woodstock, NY. Visit www.mariasebastian.com or @paperspective.

JOANELL SERRA lives and writes in Northern California. Her debut novel, The Vines We Planted, was published by Wido Publishing in May, 2018. An award-winning playwright, novelist and short story writer, she has published stories in Eclectica, Blue Lake Review, Black Fox Literary Magazine, Poydras Review and elsewhere. In 2015, she won a full scholarship to Santa Barbara's Writer's Conference and also attended the Squaw Valley Community of Writers.

CAROL SMALLWOOD's most recent poetry collection is In the Measuring (Shanti Arts, 2018). A multi-Pushcart nominee, recipient of the Albert Nelson Marquis Lifetime Achievement Award, she's founded and supports humane societies.

JOHN JAY SPEREDAKOS is a NY-based professional actor and writer with a BA from Muhlenberg College and an MFA from Rutgers University. He has appeared on and off-Broadway, in films, TV, commercials and radio dramas, and is a devoted daddy to his daughter, Calliope. Recent publications include his poems SHOULDER ME, currently an Editor's Choice and a Most Shared poem on Typishly, and MARS EVER NEARER, published last August in the debut issue of River Heron Review. More info, photos, etc. can be found on IMDb.

ALEX STANLEY is pursuing his MFA in poetry at UC Irvine. He is a former sports journalist, having worked for SportTechie and the Rio Grande SUN. He is a graduate of Boston College, where he picked up an English major, and his sports writing has been featured in Sports Illustrated. His poetry has been featured in the HCE Review (November 2018).

TRAVIS STEPHENS was raised on a dairy farm. He earned a degree at University of Wisconsin-Eau Claire, before departing for the West Coast. A sea captain, he now resides in California. Recent credits include: Stoneboat Review, Crosswinds Poetry Journal, Southword, Havik, Apeiron Review and Pennsylvania English. Online his was a Poem of the Week for Silver Needle Press and poems appeared in Ink & Voices, Rue Scribe and HCE Review.

CHARIKA SWANEPOEL is a South African poet and literary scholar. She is currently pursuing her MA. in English Poetry at North-West University. Some of her poems have appeared on platforms such as L'Éphémère Review, Glass Poetry, New Contrast, Prufrock, Aerodrome and Literator. She is founder and editor of Laurel Magazine (laurelmagazine.co.za).

JIM TRAINER publishes one collection of poetry and prose every year through Yellow Lark Press. Love&Wages is his 5th. He's also a singer-songwriter, journalist and curator of Going For The Throat—a weekly publication of cynicism, outrage, correspondence and romance.  Please visit JIMTRAINER.NET for his books, music, video and appearances.

ALIA WALL is a poet, wife, mother and lover of words. She is the 2018 winner of the Spring Pulse Poetry contest and one of the 2014/15 recipients of the Anna Pidruchney Award for Young Writers. Her poetry can also be found in The Banister, smooshed at the bottom of her purse along with PB & J sandwiches and on bits of paper scattered throughout her house. Her personal essays have been published online at The Huffington Post, as well as The Purple Fig.

JIANQING ZHENG's poems have appeared in journals including Tar River, Mississippi Review, Arkansas Review and Louisiana Literature. He is author of Enforced Rustication in the Chinese Cultural Revolution.

www.ingramcontent.com/pod-product-compliance
Lightning Source LLC
Chambersburg PA
CBHW020553030426
42337CB00013B/1072